The Beatitudes

Finding the Hand of God in Our Lives

The Beatitudes

Finding the Hand of God in Our Lives

Farley Dunn

www.ThreeSkilletPublishing.com

THIS IS A MYCHURCHNOTES.NET BOOK

PUBLISHED BY MYCHURCHNOTES.NET

www.MyChurchNotes.net

The Beatitudes: Finding the Hand of God in Our Lives/Farley Dunn – 1st ed.

This is an original work created especially by Farley Dunn for the website MyChurchNotes.net.

COPYRIGHT © 2016 BY FARLEY DUNN

All rights reserved.

THREE SKILLET
www.ThreeSkilletPublishing.com

ISBN: 978-1-943189-22-9

Table of Contents

Dedication 9
Introduction 11
Jesus begins to speak 13
The Story Behind the Story 17
Blessed Are the Poor in Spirit 27
    Matthew 5:3 (KJV) 33
Blessed Are Those Who Mourn 37
    Matthew 5:4 (KJV) 43
Blessed Are the Meek 47
    Matthew 5:5 (KJV) 55
Blessed Are Those Who Hunger and Thirst 59
    Matthew 5:6 (KJV) 67
Blessed Are the Merciful 71
    Matthew 5:7 (KJV) 79
Blessed Are the Pure in Heart 83
    Matthew 5:8 (KJV) 89
Blessed Are the Peacemakers 93
    Matthew 5:9 (KJV) 101

Blessed Are Those Who Are Persecuted........... 105
    Matthew 5:10 (KJV).............................. 111
Blessed Are You When People Insult You 115
    Matthew 5:11 (KJV).............................. 121
Coming to Christ 123

Dedication

My step-father's life was all about his family and his church, and he lived each day with gusto.

His laughter, enthusiasm, and interest in others made everyone's life better.

Thank you, J.C.

Introduction

Christ is the Church.

Yet, in his time, his ideas and teachings were controversial and contrary to the beliefs held by the prevailing religions.

The church of Jesus' day didn't welcome this man and his teachings into their carefully constructed path to religious redemption.

Even those who believed in Jesus thought he came to free the Israelites from their Roman oppressors.

It was up to Jesus to set the record straight with the Sermon on the Mount and the nine Beatitudes.

Welcome along.

Farley Dunn
Senior Writer
MyChurchNotes.net

Jesus begins to speak...

Matthew 5:1-2 (KJV)

And seeing the multitudes, [Jesus] went up into a mountain: and when he was set, his disciples came unto him: and he opened his mouth, and taught them, saying...

God opens his hand to the

Shattered Soul

— *Jesus came to offer the promise of a better life* —

The Story Behind the Story...

Capernaum.

What was special about Capernaum? Take a trip back in time. Stone houses, some multilevel, and others single story. Upper rooms, stone water wells. Stables that resemble caves, wooden corrals, stone courtyards. Even a marketplace. A typical,

The Beatitudes
Finding the Hand of God in Our Lives

roughly dressed village in the time of Jesus, this singular and pivotal location contained nothing of note that could not be found in a dozen similar villages in the region.

What was life like in Capernaum?

Located on Galilee's north shore, you might have rubbed shoulders with as many as 1,500 locals. You could have visited a simple synagogue, drawn water from deep within the earth, or used an olive press to extract oil from the fruit you gathered from the local trees.

> *You would have likely lived with your extended family members.*

The Beatitudes
Finding the Hand of God in Our Lives

The largest part of your house would have been your courtyard, containing an earthen furnace, a grain mill, and a rough set of stone steps leading to the roof. Floors generally consisted of cobbled stones, and light filtered through various openings and small windows.

You would have likely lived with your extended family members, with rooms connected through various internal passageways and shared courtyards.

There were no hygienic facilities.

For protection from the sun, your roof would consist of light wood beams covered with a thatch and mud mixture. It would

The Beatitudes
Finding the Hand of God in Our Lives

have been easy to lower a sick man through such a roof with only minor effort and minimal damage.

This is where Jesus chose to expound on the classic story of the Beatitudes, near the hometowns of a number of the apostles (Andrew, James and John, Simon Peter) as well as a storied tax collector (Matthew).

> *The ruthless Romans occupied Palestine.*

It was also in Capernaum that Jesus healed a man with the spirit of an unclean devil. According to some, Jesus selected this town as the center of his ministry as well as

The Beatitudes
Finding the Hand of God in Our Lives

formally cursed the city in Matthew 11:23, telling her that had the miracles within her borders been performed in Sodom, that city would have turned from her wicked ways.

Even the Roman Centurion had believed, coming to Capernaum to ask Jesus to heal his servant. The people of Capernaum would have done well to have followed suit.

This was where Jesus chose to ascend to the mountainside to begin his sermon.

However, the ideas he espoused were no simple words to express commonly held beliefs. The ruthless Romans occupied Palestine. If that were not bad enough, the

The Beatitudes
Finding the Hand of God in Our Lives

Jewish religion was fractured into four fundamental and very divisive groups: the Pharisees, the Sadducees, the Essenes, and the Zealots. The Pharisees and the Sadducees demanded a strict interpretation of Jewish law; the Zealots demanded freedom by any means; and the Essenes awaited the coming Messiah to free the Israelites from Roman oppression.

The common people had no words to which they could cling, none that provided them hope. Even the Ten Commandments offered things to avoid rather than the promise of a better life.

Then, in stepped Jesus, with his controversial and heraldic message spoken on the

The Beatitudes
Finding the Hand of God in Our Lives

mount. His words were the hot-bladed knife, the tightening of the fist, and the whisper of the wind.

Jesus spoke humility, charity, and brotherly love.

Jesus' kingdom was of the spirit, and in the nine Beatitudes, he offered a guidebook on how to reach that vaulted goal.

Jesus hadn't come to bring revolt against the Romans. He hadn't come to establish a kingdom on this earth. Rather, he had come to offer the promise of a better life, certainly in this world, for his teachings would make

The Beatitudes
Finding the Hand of God in Our Lives

the human condition more bearable, but more importantly, in the life to come.

Jesus' kingdom was of the spirit, and in the nine Beatitudes, he offered a guidebook on how to reach that vaulted goal. These nine verses provide the structure for the entire Book of Matthew. They provide the ideal for every Christian life.

Follow along as we break down each Beatitude into the vernacular of the day, so that we can hear Jesus' words as his listeners did. In the hearing, you will open the hand of God in your life, and you will never be the same.

Welcome along.

God opens his hand to the

Humble Hearted

*— Jesus' purpose on earth
had nothing to do with finances
or earthly possessions —*

Blessed Are the Poor in Spirit...

Matthew 5:3

What does it mean to be poor in spirit?

In Matthew 5:3, Jesus states what is to many people the most beloved verse of the Bible, where he says, Blessed are the poor in spirit, for theirs is the kingdom of heaven.

The Beatitudes
Finding the Hand of God in Our Lives

Even those who have never attended a day of church can most likely quote these thirteen words.

However, Americans have a problem with Jesus' choice of words, or one at least. The word poor flies in the face of American culture. School children are told they have a poor attitude. An automotive lemon carries a track record of poor build quality. A poorly planned house will be a bane to its owners. A poorly behaved dog will be censured repeatedly.

Let's look more closely at the word poor. Merriam-Webster tells us that poor means to lack material possessions or to be inferior in quality or value.

The Beatitudes
Finding the Hand of God in Our Lives

Why would Jesus tell those listening to be poor in anything, much less in spirit? Surely he would want them to be strong in their spirit, to winnow out all things worldly, to stand out as spiritual giants among men.

> *The key in this passage is the audience at Jesus' feet.*

Surely he meant for them to be generous, willing to donate time and effort to the emerging church.

The key in this passage is the audience at Jesus' feet. He was not speaking to the wealthy landowner, the tax collector, or the Pharisee. He was speaking to those who had

The Beatitudes
Finding the Hand of God in Our Lives

nothing, the poverty stricken, the ones who looked up to find the bottom of the barrel. These people had no claim to ego or arrogance. Everyone was better than they were. They knew the meaning of humility, to expect nothing, to have nothing, to gain nothing, to always let the other person take the higher rung on the ladder. They knew life didn't get better. That wasn't their lot.

Jesus' words were to the truly humble.

In those thirteen words, he revealed the core of his purpose on this earth. He also spoke the words the people needed to hear, words of promise and encouragement. Poverty didn't exclude them from the blessings of the kingdom. All they had to

The Beatitudes
Finding the Hand of God in Our Lives

do was come and be dependent on God. He would provide all their needs.

In modern America we can look at this in exactly the same way. The kingdom of God isn't about poverty or riches. It isn't about owning only one pair of shoes or about having the finest home in the city. The kingdom isn't about how much we give in the offering or how long we've taught a Sunday school class.

> *God's kingdom is about repentance.*

God's kingdom is about repentance. Are we willing to come with a broken heart and

The Beatitudes
Finding the Hand of God in Our Lives

a contrite spirit, to humble ourselves, to become poor in attitude before the Lord?

Then and only then we will have the kingdom of heaven.

In conclusion, Jesus' purpose on earth had nothing to do with finances or earthly possessions. He came to fulfill the needs of our hearts. Only when we can count all earthly possessions as nothing can we truly be the people he desires us to be.

The Beatitudes
Finding the Hand of God in Our Lives

Read about it in the Bible:

Matthew 5:3 (KJV)

Blessed are the poor in spirit: for theirs is the kingdom of heaven.

God opens his hand to those who

Sorrow over Sin

— *God's heart is broken over sin* —

Blessed Are Those Who Mourn...

Matthew 5:4

How can mourning be a blessing? It seems a painful reality instead, one most of us would gladly discard at the first chance.

We must first realize that our view of the world is not Jesus' view. In Matthew 5:4, he tells us that blessed are those who

The Beatitudes
Finding the Hand of God in Our Lives

mourn, for they will be comforted. The comfort part we can hold to during those valley trials when life has grown dark and weary, and it does bring hope and comfort. If for no other reason, Matthew 5:4 is one of the most valued verses in the Bible.

However, what did Jesus really mean?

This verse must be viewed in the context of the times and the crowd to which Jesus spoke. These were people to whom life was very harsh. Death was part of their daily existence, as were poverty and hard work. Their rulers were ruthless,

> *Jesus' time on earth was about the heart.*

The Beatitudes
Finding the Hand of God in Our Lives

willing to walk over the people at the least provocation.

Over the centuries, God had made glorious promises to Israel, ones that seemed to have been trampled in the dust by the Romans. Where was the grand plan that had been outlined by the prophets? Where were the mighty feats of David and the tales of glory from the time of the kings? Where was the exaltation of Israel?

Jesus came as the Messiah to God's chosen people, but his version of messianic revelation was far removed from what the people of Israel wanted from him. Jesus came because sin was rampant, because cruelty had become the norm, and because

The Beatitudes
Finding the Hand of God in Our Lives

the helpless were being abandoned by society. Jesus' time on earth was about the heart.

That was the issue he addressed.

These were people who had every reason to mourn. Yet, even as his words gave them hope, he was less concerned about the immediate sorrow of a lost son or daughter. Nor was his central concern that of oppression and poverty. He had come to comfort those who mourn, but mourn for what?

His cry was for the people to mourn over the devastation of Israel and the sin that had brought her low. When contrition

The Beatitudes
Finding the Hand of God in Our Lives

gripped the hearts of the people, then God would reach to them and comfort their pain.

Our Almighty God weeps for the sin of the nations.

The modern church is no different. Does God care when our spouse is taken from us? Of course. Does he weep with us when devastation overtakes our finances? Certainly. Is his heart broken when we go through dark days in which no hope can be found? Beyond measure.

However, that is not God's most sincere heart. God weeps for sin.

The Beatitudes
Finding the Hand of God in Our Lives

When we are broken-hearted over the state of our fallen world, and when we fall to our knees in prayer, then God's heart is broken with us, and he will be there to comfort us in our sorrow. Then and only then we will truly know the truth Jesus spoke in Matthew 5:4. Blessed are those who mourn, for they will be comforted.

In conclusion, God's heart is broken over sin. When our hearts are also broken over sin, then he will be at our side, and we will know the full measure of his comfort and blessing.

The Beatitudes
Finding the Hand of God in Our Lives

Read about it in the Bible:

Matthew 5:4 (KJV)

Blessed are they that mourn: for they shall be comforted.

God opens his hand to those who

Honor the Hurting

*— God wishes us to champion those
without hope —*

Blessed Are the Meek...

Matthew 5:5

We live in a culture that tells us to stand up for our rights, to take it like a man, and to be all we can be. How can we reconcile that with Jesus' words in Matthew 5:5?

"Blessed are the meek, for they shall

The Beatitudes
Finding the Hand of God in Our Lives

inherit the earth."

Jesus says these words just after telling the crowd on the mount that the poor will be given the kingdom of heaven, and those who mourn will be comforted. Now, in this sweeping statement, he gives his listeners the entire earth.

> *Jesus' use of the word meek was to characterize people who do not exploit others.*

However, he only promises it to the meek. That leaves many of us out, doesn't it? And anyway, why would the meek want the earth? Doesn't even the Word of God

The Beatitudes
Finding the Hand of God in Our Lives

say to be strong and of good courage? How can we read Jesus' words in Matthew 5:5 and not feel we are being given conflicting messages?

The core content of Jesus' statement centers on two of the words he chooses to use. Let's look at them for a moment.

The word *meek*:

Often we see the word meek used in connection with mice. However, consider Moses. He was described as meek. Yet, he was a leader among men, defying the pharaoh of Egypt, guiding the people of Israel across the desert, and breaking the tablets in anger when he descended from

The Beatitudes
Finding the Hand of God in Our Lives

the mountain top.

Jesus' use of the word meek was to characterize people who do not exploit others, who do not try to seize power for their own ends, and who champion the needs of the oppressed.

The word *earth*.

The earth Jesus speaks about is not the literal globe. Israel had received a promise of place from God, a land they could call their own. Now they were scattered across the known world. The hope of the people was that the Messiah would return their lands to them.

The earth Jesus speaks about is a place

The Beatitudes
Finding the Hand of God in Our Lives

that would be Israel's alone, a dwelling of security that earthly despots could not take from them.

This leads us to see Jesus' words in a new light. To rephrase this often quoted passage, try this: Inner joy will come to those who do not oppress the downtrodden, but rather lift them up in their time of need; for they will one day be gathered in heaven in the arms of the Father.

> *The inheritance God has promised us is the harvest of souls in the end time.*

In no way does this suggest we should

The Beatitudes
Finding the Hand of God in Our Lives

not strive to reclaim the fallen earth as our Christian birthright, for even as Moses looked upon the Promised Land, God assured him he would give all the land to his descendants.

That leads us to ask what God has given us for our inheritance.

The inheritance God has promised us is the harvest of souls in the end time. As Matthew 5:5 suggests, if we reach out to the poor and afflicted, many will come to know the Lord, one day rejoicing at our side in heaven, for they will see him through us.

In conclusion, in Matthew 5:5, Jesus

The Beatitudes
Finding the Hand of God in Our Lives

does not suggest that we are to be weak. Instead, he wishes us to champion those without hope, for then his kingdom will grow in strength and numbers.

The Beatitudes
Finding the Hand of God in Our Lives

Read about it in the Bible:

Matthew 5:5 (KJV)

*Blessed are the meek:
for they shall inherit the
earth.*

God opens his hand to those who

Seek His Salvation

— He desires us to need it as much as he wants to give it —

Blessed Are Those Who Hunger and Thirst...

Matthew 5:6

Forget about hunger and thirst. Those two concepts are as alien in modern America as coal-fired cook stoves and shoeing horses. In America, we need to envision something closer to home.

Gluttony.

The Beatitudes
Finding the Hand of God in Our Lives

It's true that coal-fired cook stoves still exist, as does the skill of shoeing horses. However, for most of us, we have head knowledge of them only. We have no intrinsic connection to either one.

> *We have a surplus of electronics, cars, clothing, houses, and all the other accoutrements that shout affluence to the world.*

The same is true of hunger and thirst. True, we can go to any city in our land and find people who go without food and who have limited access to plentiful clean

The Beatitudes
Finding the Hand of God in Our Lives

water. However, if truly pressed, how many of us see starving children on the television and feel our hearts bleed with anguish at the sight, all because we've been there before?

Instead, we have a surplus of electronics, cars, clothing, houses, and all the other accoutrements that shout affluence to the world. We may see it as our accepted due, but to those starving third-world children on television, America is drowning in excess. How can any Christian in America know the driving pain of true hunger and thirst?

The people of Jesus' time could relate to his words where he says in Matthew 5:6, "Blessed are those who hunger and thirst

The Beatitudes
Finding the Hand of God in Our Lives

after righteousness, for they shall be filled." They knew that when hunger and thirst — true hunger and thirst — are our constant companions, everything else becomes nonessential. The size of our television becomes a moot point. The shiniest paint job on the latest model of car can't fill our stomach. No matter how finely we dress or the house we call home, if thirst truly haunts us, we will give everything for that glass of cool, clean water.

> *If thirst truly haunts us, we will give everything for that glass of cool, clean water.*

The Beatitudes
Finding the Hand of God in Our Lives

What do we hunger and thirst for? What do we want more than anything? What is that one thing that drives us, that object for which we are willing to toss everything else aside? That promotion? A snazzier automobile? An upscale neighborhood? An increased savings account?

There's nothing wrong with any of those. However, we must turn Jesus' words to our lives. Do we want righteousness as much as we desire these other things? If so, then we must apply the same standard. Are we truly willing to cast everything else aside to obtain righteousness?

This is what Jesus is telling us. He used hunger and thirst because his listeners could

The Beatitudes
Finding the Hand of God in Our Lives

identify with those concepts. He knew hunger and thirst were central to their existence. They knew what it was like to wake up in the morning, and the only thing they could think of was where they would find that day's food and water. Everything else was secondary.

> *Jesus wants us to be filled with his spirit.*

Do we do that, wake in the morning to that overwhelming desire, one that supersedes every other thought and need? Do we ache for righteousness each day, knowing that without it we cannot survive?

The Beatitudes
Finding the Hand of God in Our Lives

Jesus wants us to be filled with his spirit. He simply desires us to need it as much as he wants to give it.

In conclusion, when we are willing to set everything else aside in order to make room for the righteousness of God, then he will give us a satisfaction that we have never before known.

The Beatitudes
Finding the Hand of God in Our Lives

Read about it in the Bible:

Matthew 5:6 (KJV)

Blessed are they which do hunger and thirst after righteousness: for they shall be filled.

God opens his hand to those who

Cherish Christian Fellowship

— *God desires us to maintain the connection that draws his body together* —

Blessed Are the Merciful...

Matthew 5:7

Think about what makes us who we are. If we regularly welcome people into our homes, what brings that out in us? If we identify with a certain social group, is there a reason we gravitate that direction?

The Beatitudes
Finding the Hand of God in Our Lives

In Matthew 5:7, Jesus spoke from the mount to a gathering of people who soaked up his every word. When he said to them, "Blessed are the merciful, for they shall be shown mercy," he pinned them right in the core of who they were.

In our lives, it's easy to insulate ourselves from the realities of those around us.

Many years ago, I went with my mother to visit the gravesite of her twin sons who had died at an early age decades before. They were born many years before I came along, and I only knew of them through

The Beatitudes
Finding the Hand of God in Our Lives

pictures and anecdotal stories. When we reached the gravesite, I asked her if visiting the grave brought back many memories. She turned to me without a word, and tears were running down her face.

> *Blessed are those who host a church gathering, for they will be invited to others' houses.*

Over the years she made a personal ministry of searching out those who had lost loved ones, working to ease that time for them. When I asked her why she went to all that trouble, she told me that she felt her experience gave her an affinity for those

The Beatitudes
Finding the Hand of God in Our Lives

people, and she understood their pain as only one who has lost a child can.

She made her loss into a ministry to help other people in like situations.

The people to whom Jesus spoke were from a stratum of society that knew what it was to need help from others. Their lives were filled with mistakes, abusive overlords, and worldly situations over which they had no control. When the occasional time of bounty came their way, they were quick to

> *Blessed are those who invite visitors to lunch, for they will make new friends.*

The Beatitudes
Finding the Hand of God in Our Lives

understand what it meant to be in need, and they were quick to share. In return, they hoped others would do the same.

In our lives, it's easy to insulate ourselves from the realities of those around us. Our bills are automated, we use the self-check aisle at the supermarket, and we drive

> *Blessed are those who pray for those in need, for others will hold them up in prayer.*

through the bank, never interacting with more than the teller's voice. We may email our neighbors, rather than take the time to walk next door. Now, even church comes

The Beatitudes
Finding the Hand of God in Our Lives

into our homes, and we never have to shake another hand ever again.

God desires us to maintain the connection that draws his body together. Jesus said that blessed are the merciful, but we can take it further. Blessed are those who host a church gathering, for they will be invited to others' houses. Blessed are those who invite visitors to lunch, for they will make new friends. Blessed are those who pray for those in need, for others will hold them up in prayer.

Yet this does not mean to congregate with only those of like mind. It means that if we congregate, we will become of like mind.

The Beatitudes
Finding the Hand of God in Our Lives

In conclusion, if we want to find Jesus in ourselves, look for Jesus in others. Then spend time with those people, and soon Jesus will be all that people see in us.

The Beatitudes
Finding the Hand of God in Our Lives

Read about it in the Bible:

Matthew 5:7 (KJV)

Blessed are the merciful: for they shall obtain mercy.

God opens his hand to the

Committed Christian

— Jesus was kind to the down-trodden, patient to the helpless, and generous to those in need —

Blessed Are the Pure in Heart...

Matthew 5:8

We equate our hearts with love. However, where do "will" and "intent" originate? The head? Do we feel in one location and think in another?

To understand what Jesus meant in Matthew 5:8, we first must understand the

The Beatitudes
Finding the Hand of God in Our Lives

Old Testament view of the heart. If not, then Jesus' words, "Blessed are the pure in heart; for they will see God," is only of interest to those with romantic leanings.

In the Old Testament, the heart is the inner source for the choices we make, for our will, for those moments of intent that spring from us, whether planned or spontaneous. It's the location of our innermost desires, which may very well be romantic, but which are more often not.

> *When we are born again, our spiritual hearts are transformed.*

The Beatitudes
Finding the Hand of God in Our Lives

The heart is what reflects what we truly are inside. In Genesis we read that it is constantly selfish, causing grief to God. In one place in Matthew, Jesus says it defiles people with evil thoughts, impure desires, and the like.

The next time we look in a mirror, we need to look closely and see if we can find our heart. Oh, we will not find it in the slant of our forehead, or the cast of our eyes. It will not be in the cut of our chin, or the layering of our haircut. No, we will have to look deeper to find our heart.

Instead, imagine the driver of the car that cut us off on the way home from work. How did he see our response? Picture the

The Beatitudes
Finding the Hand of God in Our Lives

woman in front of us the last time we checked out at the grocery store. When she spent more time in conversation with the clerk than in moving her bags to her cart, how deep was our frown? When our co-worker infringed on our rights, and we were left to cover what he left undone, how did we greet him the following morning?

We have Jesus' example to model our hearts on. He was kind to the downtrodden, patient to the helpless, and generous to those in need. The only time he felt anger was when his father's house was being treated with disdain, and he championed respect for God.

When we are born again, our spiritual

The Beatitudes
Finding the Hand of God in Our Lives

hearts are transformed. So are our will and our intent. The decisions we make are different, and we begin to show those things that please God: love; mercy; desire for righteousness and justice.

If we have a pure heart, our thoughts and intentions are unblemished by sin.

If we please God, then we will see God when we look in our mirror, for we will reflect him. We will still see our forehead, our eyes, and our chin. However, we will know that others have seen God in our actions, for they have seen the results of

The Beatitudes
Finding the Hand of God in Our Lives

our pure heart.

In conclusion, if we have a pure heart, our thoughts and intentions are unblemished by sin. Our will is pleasing to God, and at the end of time, he will welcome us into his everlasting arms.

The Beatitudes
Finding the Hand of God in Our Lives

Read about it in the Bible:

Matthew 5:8 (KJV)

Blessed are the pure in heart: for they shall see God.

God opens his hand to offer

Deliverance for the Downtrodden

— God desires a reconciliation of the broken relationship between him and his creation —

Blessed Are the Peacemakers...

Matthew 5:9

Is it possible to know true peace, whether in our families, in our cities, or across our world?

Even in the church we find dissention and strife. If Christians cannot find peace among themselves, what hope is there for

The Beatitudes
Finding the Hand of God in Our Lives

the rest of the world? Yet, in Matthew 5:9, Jesus clearly says, "Blessed are the peacemakers, for they shall be called the sons of God."

When we pray the sinner's prayer, and we accept God into our hearts, the Word tells us that we become the children of the Almighty Father. We are wrapped in the arms of God, and we have become a family. Years ago, church members regularly greeted each other as brother and sister. That may have gone out

> *If we are reconciled, we have a former relationship restored.*

The Beatitudes
Finding the Hand of God in Our Lives

of style, but the concept of the church as a family has not.

So, in this passage Jesus must be telling us something different. Let's look at what he means by his use of the words "peacemakers" and "sons."

First, turn to "peacemakers."

Merriam-Webster tells us that a peacemaker makes peace – naturally! – by reconciliation. If we are reconciled, we have a former relationship restored.

That leads us to yet another question. What relationship has been broken? In Genesis, the disobedience of Adam and Eve broke God's perfect relationship between

The Beatitudes
Finding the Hand of God in Our Lives

man and the world around him, and between man and God. For that reason, there will be no true peace on earth until God returns at the end of time to create a new heaven and a new earth.

> *A son can be an offspring, adopted, or simply a descendant.*

Next, take a look at "sons."

Merriam-Webster gives us three applicable meanings that might apply to this verse. A son can be an offspring, adopted, or simply a descendant.

Does Jesus use one of these meanings

The Beatitudes
Finding the Hand of God in Our Lives

specifically, or can his words apply to all three?

In the Old Testament, the angels were referred to as the sons of God. The Word

> *If we allow God's love to draw unbelievers to Christ, we will become peacemakers.*

tells us God created them. In Genesis, God created Adam from the dust of the ground. However, in the New Testament, the phrase comes to mean someone who has accepted salvation. He creates in us a new heart.

The peace of God is not the give and take of compromise or the ending of

The Beatitudes
Finding the Hand of God in Our Lives

hostilities among nations. Rather, the peace of God comes from his redemptive plan. As one of Adam's descendants, when we embrace salvation, we not only become a spiritual offspring, but we are adopted into the spiritual family that makes up the body of believers.

If we allow God's love to shine through us, drawing unbelievers to Christ, we will become peacemakers, for we will have played a part in the reconciliation of God with his creation. Then we will truly be a son of the Most

> *The peace God desires is not a peace among the nations.*

The Beatitudes
Finding the Hand of God in Our Lives

High Father, for we will be like him.

In conclusion, the peace God desires is not a peace among the nations. Rather, he desires a reconciliation of the broken relationship between him and his creation.

The Beatitudes
Finding the Hand of God in Our Lives

Read about it in the Bible:

Matthew 5:9 (KJV)

Blessed are the peacemakers: for they shall be called the children of God.

God opens his hand to those desiring

Moral Maturity

— *When we uphold God's moral standards, he will reward us with the kingdom of heaven* —

Blessed Are Those Who Are Persecuted...

Matthew 5:10

Is there a difference between right and righteous? What should those words mean to us today?

Matthew 5:10 tells us that blessed are those who are persecuted because of righteousness, for theirs is the kingdom of

The Beatitudes
Finding the Hand of God in Our Lives

heaven.

In an interview, singer Josh Turner recounted his first brush with fame. He had just debuted his album, *Long Black Train*, to national acclaim. On tour, he set the moral standards for those with him very high, and he refused to compromise those standards. He told of how he was criticized for his beliefs, despite the fact that his musical success was unprecedented for a newcomer.

Was Josh Turner right, or was he righteous?

John the Baptist called for a moral change in the leadership of his day, and he

The Beatitudes
Finding the Hand of God in Our Lives

received the ultimate criticism. He had his head removed from his body. Where was his kingdom of heaven?

In our daily walk, for the Christian as well as the unbeliever, persecution will hit us from all sides. Jesus found opposition because his call to righteousness demanded that people turn from their willful ways, and for them to embrace his message of moral change. He died painfully for his beliefs.

> *We can be right, and still not be in the will of God.*

We have laws in our land to tell us the right thing to do, directions to tell us the right way to make

The Beatitudes
Finding the Hand of God in Our Lives

things, and advisors to tell us the right way to invest our money. We see people on the news who champion causes, saving the spotted owl or protecting endangered habitats. Those who champion children's rights are considered heroes.

What about those who tell us the right way to live? Missionaries and Sunday school teachers. Pastors. Christian grandparents. Musicians with morals. Those who refuse to stoop to the world's standards just to step one rung higher on the ladder of success.

Our world is a fallen world, and our earthly man continually cries out for worldly pleasure. When Christians promote

The Beatitudes
Finding the Hand of God in Our Lives

moral behavior, it often conflicts with the desires of our sinful nature.

We can be right, and still not be in the will of God. Just because we are right in what we do does not mean we will see the kingdom of heaven.

> *When we uphold God's standards even when it's difficult to do so, then God will be at our side, and he will draw us to him.*

However, when we are righteous, when we uphold God's standards even when it's difficult to do so, then God will be at our side, and he will draw us to him. Then we shall see the kingdom of

The Beatitudes
Finding the Hand of God in Our Lives

God, and we shall be with him in his glory.

In conclusion, persecution comes to everyone, believer and unbeliever alike. However, when we uphold God's moral standards, he will reward us with the kingdom of heaven.

The Beatitudes
Finding the Hand of God in Our Lives

Read about it in the Bible:

Matthew 5:10 (KJV)

Blessed are they which are persecuted for righteousness' sake: for theirs is the kingdom of heaven.

God opens his hand to those

Pierced with Pain

— Even when our pain seems too great for words, Jesus promises he will be with us in our darkest hours —

Blessed Are You When People Insult You...

Matthew 5:11

Think of the last time someone hurt your feelings. It was probably someone you held dear to your heart.

Today, we casually criticize people on television, remark on billboards we dislike, and discuss the moral ineptitude of our

The Beatitudes
Finding the Hand of God in Our Lives

politicians with aplomb. Our words rarely impact those to whom they're directed, and once we go on to other topics, our comments are forgotten.

An insult from someone who barely knows us carries little weight.

During his time on earth, Jesus was condemned by the Jewish leaders, who accused him before the Roman authorities of treasonous acts. Just before the crucifixion, Peter denied him three times. Which of these acts hurt Jesus more?

An insult from someone who barely knows us carries little weight. An insult

The Beatitudes
Finding the Hand of God in Our Lives

from a close companion, a spouse, or a child can cut us to the quick. When a co-worker we have labored with for years falsely accuses us of wrong-doing in the workplace, the sting may haunt us for years, souring our relationship.

In Matthew 5:11, Jesus says that we are blessed when people insult us and falsely accuse us of evil because of him; and that we will see our reward in heaven. He wraps up the Beatitudes with a statement that impacts us at our most vulnerable level.

Our emotions.

The crowd to whom Jesus spoke was used to having cruel words thrown at them.

The Beatitudes
Finding the Hand of God in Our Lives

The Jewish people had long ago lost their supremacy in the social order. They were the underdogs of their society.

That suggests Jesus' statement spoke of something deeper.

An insult from a close companion, a spouse, or a child can cut us to the quick.

The true insult, the accusation that slices us to the core, is the one that comes from a trusted friend or family member. When those whom we trust most criticize our Christian morals, or when we find we have been deceived by a confidante, the blow often staggers us, and we cannot

The Beatitudes
Finding the Hand of God in Our Lives

understand the reason for the attack. It seems to come out of the blue.

This is the insult Jesus spoke of.

When a Christian friend forsakes the church and levels ugly insults our direction, or when our spouse attacks our relationship with Jesus, the wound we receive can create a scar that may follow us for all of our days. Even turning it over to Jesus may not totally heal the damage that's been done.

However, there is one thing we can count on. When we let Jesus' love shine through us, even when the pain seems greater than we can bear, the peace of God will be ours, for he has promised that he

The Beatitudes
Finding the Hand of God in Our Lives

will never leave us nor forsake us.

In conclusion, the cruelest insults seem to come from those we hold closest to our hearts. Even when our pain seems too great for words, Jesus promises he will be with us in our darkest hours, and through him, we will have a great reward.

The Beatitudes
Finding the Hand of God in Our Lives

Read about it in the Bible:

Matthew 5:11 (KJV)

Blessed are ye, when men shall revile you, and persecute you, and shall say all manner of evil against you falsely, for my sake.

Coming to Christ

In Three Easy Steps

If you do not know Christ as your personal savior, there is no better time than the present to turn your life over to him.

> ➢ Step 1 is to admit that you are human, God is God, and you need his grace.
> ➢ Step 2 is to place your belief in him. You must accept that he is the Son of the Eternal God, and through his death on the cross, he can give you new life.
> ➢ Step 3 is to turn from your previous ways and receive the hope of Jesus' power in you.

Fill in the following information as a testament to your decision to accept Jesus as your Savior.

I, _____, accept Jesus
      print your full name

as my personal savior on _____.
                                 today's date

_____
            your signature

Look for these additional topics on the *MyChurchNotes.net website:*

2 Timothy
Beatitudes
Discipleship
Evangelism
Faith
Family
Healing
Hope
Kingdom of God
Money
Prayer
Relationships
Repentance
Salvation
Worship

MyChurchNotes.net is a faith-based ministry founded on a belief in the Father, the Son, and the Holy Spirit. All MyChurchNotes.net articles are based on Scripture and created especially for MyChurchNotes.net.

Our Mission Statement is to take the Word of God into all the nations, and proclaim that he is Lord!

If you enjoyed

The Beatitudes: Finding the Hand of God in Our Lives,

please visit us at our website:

www.MyChurchNotes.net

We look forward to hearing from you.

Website and Publication Powered by:

Freedom in Imagination, Planning, and Execution - Never One of the Crowd

Bright Herd . . . for All Your Website and
Media Design Needs.
www.brightherd.com
contact@brightherd.com

www.ingramcontent.com/pod-product-compliance
Lightning Source LLC
Chambersburg PA
CBHW061445040426
42450CB00007B/1229